Awesome Animals

Alison Hawes

FULL FLIGHT

Badger Publishing Limited
Oldmedow Road,
Hardwick Industrial Estate,
King's Lynn PE30 4JJ
Telephone: 01438 791037

www.badgerlearning.co.uk

2 4 6 8 10 9 7 5 3

Awesome Animals ISBN 978-1-84424-823-0 (second edition) 2013

Text © Alison Hawes 2006
Complete work © Badger Publishing Limited 2006

Publisher: Susan Ross
Senior Editor: Danny Pearson
Designer: Fiona Grant

Photos: Cover image: Image Source / Rex Features
Page 4: Dita Alangkara/AP/Press Association Images
Page 5: DAVE THOMPSON/AP/Press Association Images
Page 7: Nature Picture Library / Rex Features
Page 8: Franco Banfi/Solent News / Rex Features
Page 9: Gerard Lacz / Rex Features
Page 10: Stock Connection Blue / Alamy
Page 11: KIKE CALVO/AP/Press Association Images
Page 12: Vnoucek, F./DPA/Press Association Images
Page 13: Rex Features
Page 14: Rex Features
Page 15: Mark Mitchell / Rex Features
Page 16: KOJI SASAHARA/AP/Press Association Images
Page 17: Design Pics Inc / Rex Features
Page 18: Image Broker / Rex Features
Page 19: Design Pics Inc / Rex Features
Page 20: CTK CZECH NEWS AGENCY/Czech News Agency/Press Association Images
Page 21: John Pitcher / Design Pics Inc. / Rex Features
Page 22: Design Pics Inc / Rex Features
Page 23: Design Pics Inc / Rex Features
Page 24: Wilfredo Lee/AP/Press Association Images
Page 25: IS2 from Image Source / Alamy
Page 26: Image Broker / Rex Features
Page 27: Image Source / Rex Features
Page 28: Tony Heald / Nature Picture Library / Rex Features
Page 29: Eye Ubiquitous/Press Association Images
Page 30: Mike Hill / Alamy
Page 31: KeystoneUSA-ZUMA / Rex Features

Attempts to contact all copyright holders have been made.
If any omitted would care to contact Badger Learning, we will be happy to make appropriate arrangements.

Contents

1. Awesome animals of the rainforest

Komodo dragons are the heaviest lizards on the planet! They have sharp, claws and sharp jagged teeth to kill their prey. They also have poisonous spit! So even if an animal escapes from the dragon's jaws, it will die within 24 hours from blood poisoning.

Awesome fact

Komodo dragons can be as long as a car!

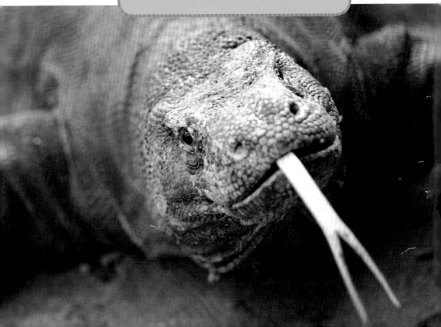

Baby Komodo dragons spend their first year of life up in the forest trees.

They don't come down to the forest floor until they are at least a metre long. This is because adult Komodo dragons will eat their own young!

Awesome fact
Komodo dragons have been known to attack or even kill people.

This is a vampire bat.

Vampire bats live in the understorey of the rainforest. This is the part of the forest below the treetops.

Awesome fact
Baby bats are called pups!

Every night the bats leave their roost and fly off in search of food. As they glide through the air, they look for large animals and birds, so they can drink their blood.

They make a little cut in their victim's skin and then lap up the blood with their tongues. Quite often their victim doesn't even wake up!

Awesome fact
Vampire bats have even been known to drink human blood!

Anacondas live by the riverbanks in the rainforest. When they sense danger they like to slip into the water to escape.

They eat big animals like deer and crocodiles as well as fish and birds. They squeeze their victims until they stop breathing. Then they swallow them whole.

Awesome fact

Anacondas are the biggest snakes in the world. They can be as long as a bus!

This is a red-eyed tree frog.

Being green helps the red-eyed tree frog blend in with tree leaves.

If the frog is spotted by a predator then it flashes its colourful eyes and legs in order to confuse it long enough for the frog to escape.

Awesome fact

Tree frogs have suction disks on their fingers and toes that help them stick to leaves.

This rainforest bird is the hoatzin.
It is also called the stinkbird. This is
because it smells like a cowpat!

Baby hoatzins are born with claws on
their wings. These are to help them climb
trees until they are big enough to fly.

2. Awesome animals of the sea

You are looking into the jaws of a great white shark!

Great white sharks live in coastal areas of the sea. They eat big animals like seals.

Awesome fact

After eating a seal or a sea lion the great white shark can last up to two months without another big meal.

Great whites are the biggest meat eating sharks. They can smell their prey a long way away. They can move towards their victims at speeds of up to 43 miles an hour.

Once they have caught their food, they bite off big chunks of flesh and swallow them whole. They cannot chew.

Awesome fact
A shark cannot blink!

This big, ugly fish is an anglerfish. It lives deep down in the sea where there is little light. It eats many different types of fish.

A female anglerfish can 'fish' for her food. Fish are attracted to the light on the end of the 'fishing rod' on her head.

Then as they come close – she eats them!

Awesome fact

Anglerfish have big mouths. They can eat fish that are bigger than they are!

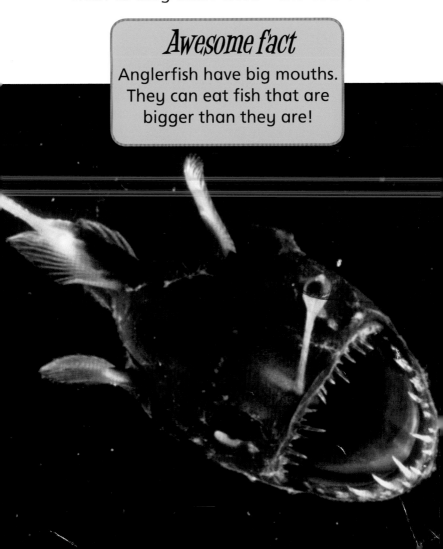

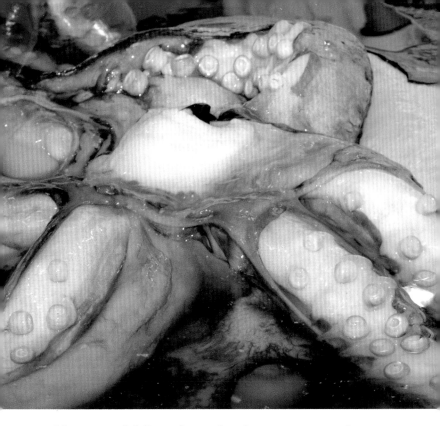

Giant squid live deep in the ocean and are rarely seen.

They eat different kinds of fish and other smaller squid.

Awesome fact
Giant squid have the biggest eyes in the world!

The giant squid has eight legs and two extra-long tentacles for catching its prey. There are suckers on the ends of each tentacle for grabbing its prey.

Once it has grabbed its prey, the squid eats it with its parrot-like beak.

Awesome fact

Giant squid are the biggest invertebrates on Earth!

A porcupine fish is covered in sharp spines.
It has sharp teeth to eat the shellfish it
feeds on.

When it is afraid it can puff itself up until
it is two or three times bigger. It does this
by drawing air or water into a sac in its body.

When the danger has gone it returns to its
normal size.

3. Awesome animals of the desert

Most common scorpions live in the desert.

They live under rocks and grab their prey with big claws. They feed on insects and other small animals like spiders.

Awesome fact

This scorpion carries its babies on its back!

Most scorpions are poisonous.

They use poison to kill their prey and to protect themselves. They have a barb at the end of their tail. They use this to inject their poison.

Awesome fact

Some scorpion stings can kill people!

This huge spider is a Mexican red-kneed tarantula.

It lives under rocks and sand in the desert. Its prey is small animals like frogs and snakes.

Awesome fact

Some tarantulas live for 30 years!

Tarantulas shed their skin several times a year so they can grow. They cannot feed for a week after moulting as their new fangs are too soft.

Awesome fact

A tarantula can kill its prey with the poison in its fangs!

Gila monsters live in rocks and sand in the desert.

They are one of the few poisonous lizards in the world. They eat small animals like birds and frogs but can go without food for a long time because their tail is full of fat.

Gila monsters have a thick forked tongue and sharp teeth. Their skin is covered in scales with patches of colour.

They also have big claws for digging.

Awesome fact

Gila monsters spend most of their time underground, only coming out to feed or sit in the sun.

There are about 24 different kinds of rattlesnake in the world and they all have a rattle at the end of their tail.

They shake the rattle to warn predators away.

Rattlesnakes store their venom in glands behind their eyes. When they bite their prey, poison is squeezed into their fangs from the glands.

4. Awesome animals of the grasslands

Warthogs are a type of wild pig.

They use their snouts to dig up roots to eat. Warthogs look fierce but they are more likely to run away than fight!

But if they are cornered they will use their tusks as weapons to protect themselves.

Awesome fact
Warthogs can run at 30 miles an hour.

Hippos live in the grasslands of Africa.

They like to live near watering holes and are excellent underwater swimmers. In fact, their name means river horse.

Awesome fact
Baby hippos are born underwater!

Hippos stay in the water during the day but come out in the evening to feed on the grass.

They are one of the most dangerous animals in Africa. They kill more people each year than any other African land animal.

Awesome fact

Hippos look heavy and slow but they can outrun a human.

Black rhinos live in the grasslands of Africa and they eat trees and bushes.

Like hippos, they come out at night to feed. During the day they stay in the shade or wallow in mud.

Awesome fact
When rhinos roll in mud, the mud protects their skin like sun cream.

Black rhinos cannot see very well but they have excellent hearing and a good sense of smell.

They have two sharp horns which they use to protect themselves and their young.

Awesome fact
Black rhinos are not black, they are grey!

Lions live in groups call prides.

The female lions look after the cubs and do most of the hunting. There may be lots of females in a pride but usually no more than two males.

Awesome fact

A lion's roar can be heard five miles away!

When a lioness catches food, the male
lions eat first, then the females and finally
the cubs get what is left. The males can
eat up to 27 kilos of meat at one meal.

Awesome fact
When lions walk their heels
don't touch the ground!

Index